My Favorite Dogs

BOXER

Jinny Johnson

A+

Smart Apple Media

Published by Smart Apple Media
P.O. Box 1329
Mankato, MN 56002

Printed in the United States of America,
at Corporate Graphics in North Mankato, Minnesota.

Designed by Hel James
Edited by Mary-Jane Wilkins

Library of Congress Cataloging-in-Publication Data

Johnson, Jinny, 1949-
  Boxer / by Jinny Johnson.
     p. cm. -- (My favorite dogs)
  Includes index.
  Summary: "Describes the care, training, and rearing of the boxer. Also explains
the boxer's unique characteristics and history"--Provided by publisher.
  ISBN 978-1-59920-840-4 (hardcover, library bound)
  1. Boxer (Dog breed)--Juvenile literature. I. Title.
  SF429.B75J64 2013
  636.73--dc23
                            2012012139

Photo acknowledgements
t = top, b = bottom
page 1 guillermo77/Shutterstock; 3 Jeff Thrower/Shutterstock; 4 Karen
Givens/Shutterstock; 5 AnetaPics/Shutterstock; 6 Jupiterimages/Thinkstock;
7 Hemera/Thinkstock; 8-9 Lebedinski Vladislav/Shutterstock; 11 Whytock/
Shutterstock; 12 iStockphoto/Thinkstock; 13t iStockphoto/Thinkstock,
b Linn Currie/Shutterstock; 14 Joy Brown/Shutterstock; 15 cynoclub/
Shutterstock; 16 Hemera/Thinkstock; 17 Jana Behr/Shutterstock, b Hemera/
Thinkstock; 18 Mars Evis/Shutterstock; 19 Anna Hoychuk/Shutterstock;
20 Hemera/Thinkstock; 21 iStockphoto/Thinkstock; 22-23 AnetaPics/
Shutterstock; 23 Lenkadan/Shutterstock
Cover Nate A./Shutterstock

DAD0504a
112012
9 8 7 6 5 4 3 2

Contents

I'm a Boxer!

I'm handsome, loving, and fun to be with. I'll be your loyal friend, playmate, and protector.

What I Need

I'm bouncy and full of energy, so I need plenty of exercise every day. I like to run and play games, and I love to clown around sometimes, too.

I'm happiest when I'm with people and I like being petted and cuddled. I get sad if I'm left alone too long.

The Boxer

Smooth short coat

Tail often docked (trimmed) at birth

Tight skin

Color:
fawn or brindle (brownish with streaks of other colors) with white

Height:
21½–25 inches (54½–63½ cm)

Weight:
55–70 pounds (25–32 kg)

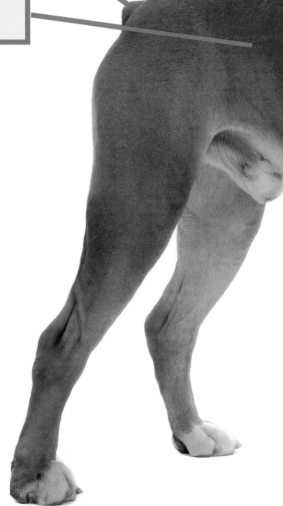

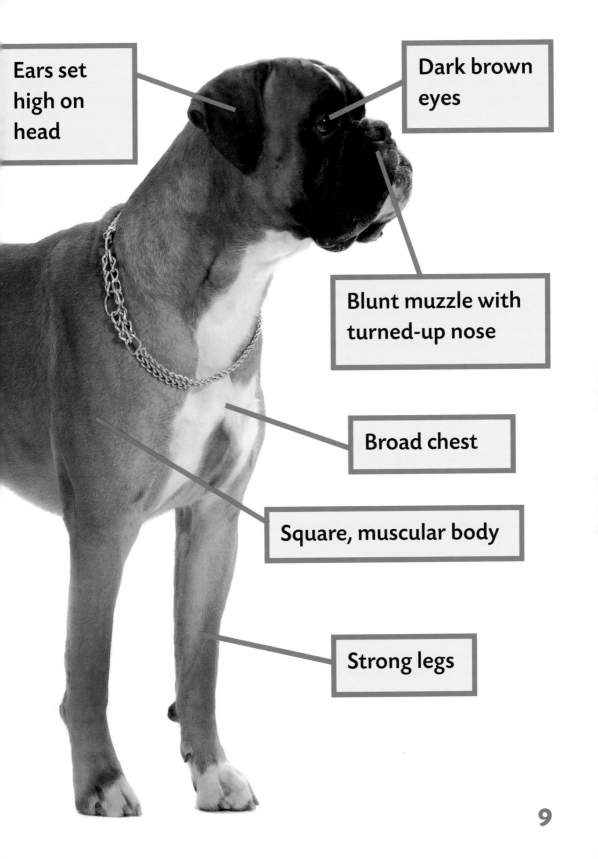

Ears set high on head

Dark brown eyes

Blunt muzzle with turned-up nose

Broad chest

Square, muscular body

Strong legs

9

All About Boxers

Boxers are related to bulldogs. They were first bred in Germany in the 1800s for hunting animals such as deer.

Boxers are not used for hunting today, but they are brave, intelligent animals. They make good guard dogs, and will defend the family.

Growing Up

A boxer pup is an adorable bundle of energy that needs lots of attention

A boxer pup will miss her mom when she first goes to her new home. Be extra kind and gentle with your pup and she will soon learn to love her human family.

Be warned—
boxer pups love
to chew, so give
your puppy
plenty of toys.

Training Your Boxer

Boxers want to please their owners, but they can be stubborn so need careful training. Start training your boxer when she's young and always show her who is boss. A well-trained boxer is a happy boxer.

Boxers are athletic dogs and they perform well at agility trials.

Working Dogs

These dogs are intelligent, as well as strong, and often become working dogs. Boxers carried messages in wartime, and were one of the first breeds to be trained as police dogs.

Boxers also work as seeing-eye dogs and service dogs.

They love
to help
and protect
people.

Good Company

Many boxer owners say their dogs are great company for all the family. Boxers show their feelings in their faces. Look at those eyes and that wrinkly forehead!

Boxers are very
good at sensing
moods. They love
to play when their owner
is happy, but they will cuddle
up and comfort you when they
feel you need it.

Your Healthy Boxer

A boxer has short hair and her coat only needs brushing once a week. She doesn't need a bath often either, unless she has rolled in something smelly.

Boxers do not like very warm weather, so don't let your dog run too far and overheat on summer days.

Boxers can have hip problems, so have a puppy checked before buying. Get your boxer used to having her teeth cleaned when she is young, and brush them regularly.

Caring for Your Boxer

You and your family must think very carefully before buying a boxer. She may live as long as 11 years. Every day your dog must have food, water, and exercise, as well as lots of love and care. She will also need to be taken to the vet for checks and vaccinations. When you go out or away, you must plan for your dog to be looked after.

Useful Words

agility competitions
Events where dogs run around courses with obstacles and jumps.

breed
A particular type of dog.

vaccinations
injections given by the vet to protect your dog against certain illnesses.

Index